Usborne
Build your own
CARS
Sticker Book

T0015658

Illustrated by John Shirley

Designed by Marc Maynard
Written by Simon Tudhope

Contents

You'll find
all the stickers in
the middle of the book.

Super car

This road car comes alive on the track.
With quick-shift gears and a super-charged
engine, it's built to be driven fast.

Statistics

- **Top speed:** 185mph
- **0-60:** 4.6s
- **Horsepower:** 470hp
- **Engine:** 6 liter V12

Le Mans Prototype

This machine takes part in one of motorsport's ultimate endurance tests: Le Mans 24 Hours. It tears around a track for a whole day and night, on full throttle nearly all the way.

Statistics

- **Top speed:** 210mph
- **0-60:** 3.5s
- **Horsepower:** 680hp
- **Engine:** 3.4 liter V8

Pro Mod drag racer

Drag cars are built for blistering speed over short distances. Fitted with a supercharged engine, this is a seriously fast machine.

Statistics

- **Top speed:** 260mph
- **0-60:** 1.1s
- **Horsepower:** 3,500hp
- **Engine:** 8.6 liter V8

SUV

This sports utility vehicle is equipped with four-wheel drive and deep suspension, so it can power up rugged mountain tracks.

Statistics

- **Top speed:** 125mph
- **0-60:** 8.6s
- **Horsepower:** 290hp
- **Engine:** 3.6 liter V6 diesel

Hot rod

If Dr. Frankenstein had created a car, it would've been a hot rod. Bolted together from parts of different vehicles, this drag racer is monstrously fast.

Statistics

- **Top speed:** 140mph
- **0-60:** 5.5s
- **Horsepower:** 500hp
- **Engine:** 5.8 liter V8

Convertible car

Like a car from the movies, this machine is built to thunder down a desert highway, heading straight for the sunset.

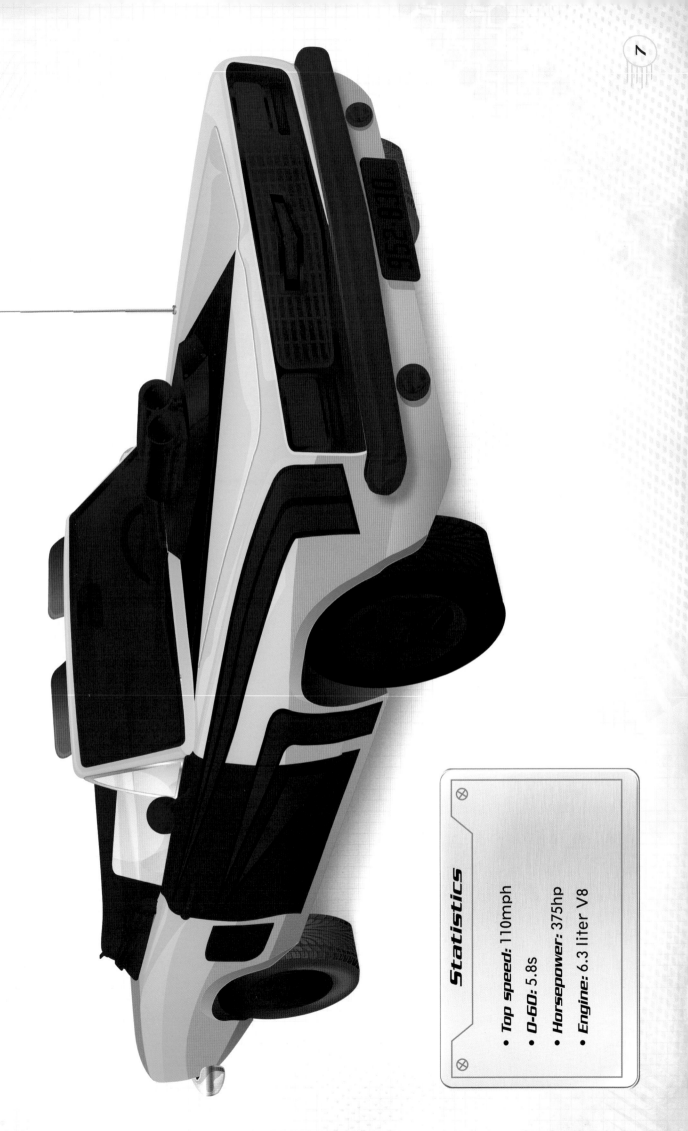

Statistics

- **Top speed:** 110mph
- **0-60:** 5.8s
- **Horsepower:** 375hp
- **Engine:** 6.3 liter V8

Hyper car

Hyper cars are like superheroes: they do everything normal cars can do, only faster, harder and with a lot more style.

Statistics

- **Top speed:** 220mph
- **0-60:** 2.8s
- **Horsepower:** 695hp
- **Engine:** 6.5 liter V12

Formula One car

An F1 car is the peak of automobile technology. It's fast, loud and sweeps around corners like a heat-seeking missile.

Statistics

- **Top speed:** 215mph
- **0-60:** 2.5s
- **Horsepower:** 1000hp
- **Engine:** 1.6 liter V6

Rocket car

With a rocket in the middle and a jet engine on either side, this machine is faster than a speeding bullet. So strap yourself in and hold on tight, it's going to be a supersonic ride...

Statistics

- **Top speed:** 1,000mph
- **0-60:** 2.5s
- **Horsepower:** 130,000hp
- **Engine:** 2 jet engines, 1 rocket

Muscle car

An American classic. Muscle cars are mid-sized machines pumped up with a huge V8 engine, for pure straight line acceleration.

Statistics

- **Top speed:** 120mph
- **0-60:** 4.1s
- **Horsepower:** 425hp
- **Engine:** 7 liter V8

4x4

Tearing through terrain that other cars can't handle, this four-wheel drive is one seriously tough piece of machinery.

Statistics

- **Top speed:** 105mph
- **0-60:** 7.8s
- **Horsepower:** 300hp
- **Engine:** 3.6 liter V6

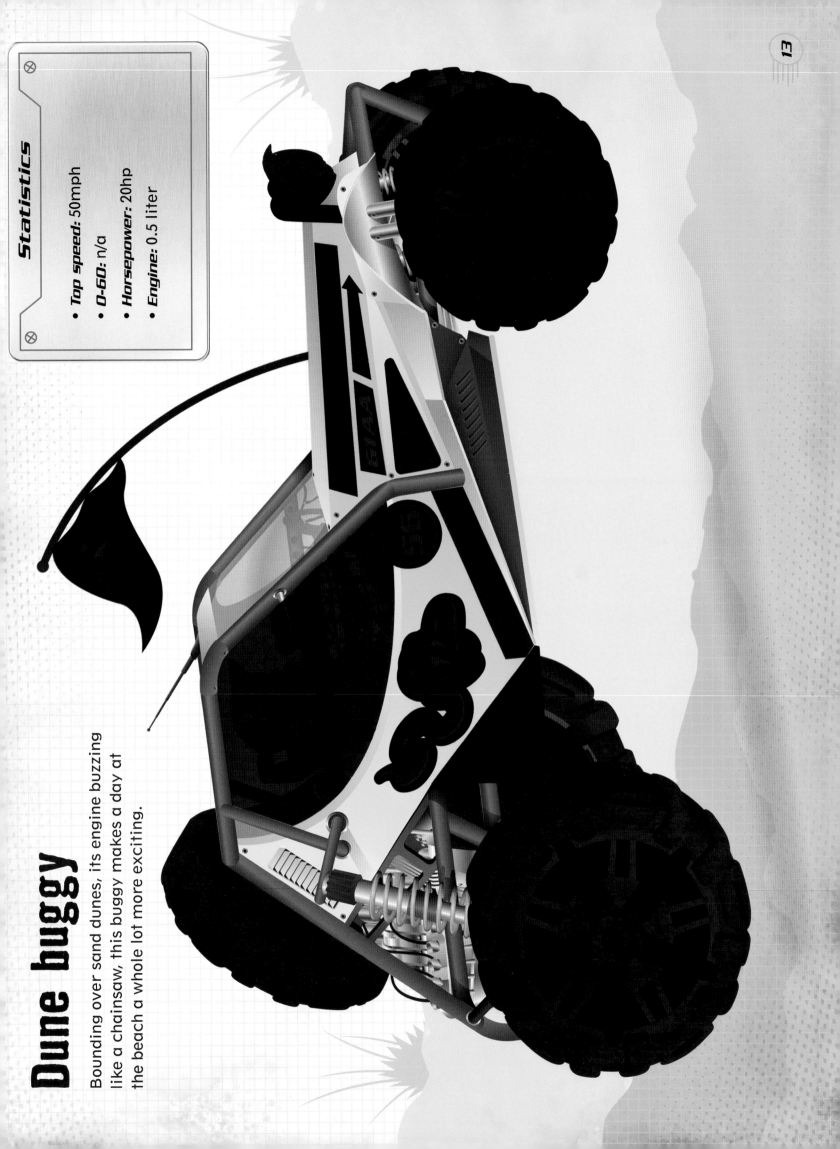

Statistics

- **Top speed:** 50mph
- **0-60:** n/a
- **Horsepower:** 20hp
- **Engine:** 0.5 liter

Dune buggy

Bounding over sand dunes, its engine buzzing like a chainsaw, this buggy makes a day at the beach a whole lot more exciting.

Demolition car

To the sound of revving engines and tortured metal, these demolition derby cars smash into each other until just one is still moving.

Statistics

- **Top speed:** 80mph
- **0-60:** 16s
- **Horsepower:** 250hp
- **Engine:** 5 liter V8

Vintage racing car

Before safety regulations, before electronics, even before seatbelts, racing was for real daredevils. Drivers got covered with oil and dirt, and one mistake could mean serious trouble.

Statistics

- **Top speed:** 110mph
- **0-60:** 10s
- **Horsepower:** 160hp
- **Engine:** 2.3 liter straight-8

Stock car racer

This car takes part in the NASCAR Sprint Cup, the top motorsport series in America. The racers jostle for position around a banked track, and a spectacular crash is only a wheel-clip away.

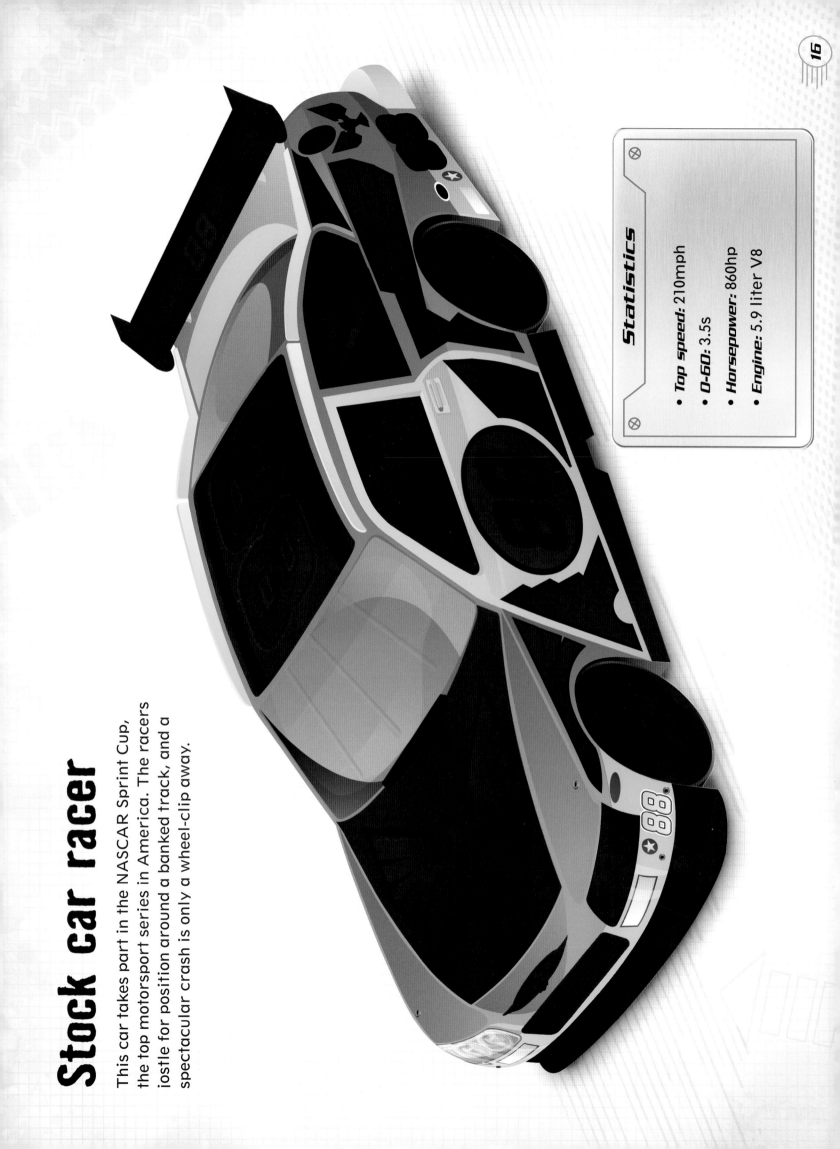

Statistics

- **Top speed:** 210mph
- **0-60:** 3.5s
- **Horsepower:** 860hp
- **Engine:** 5.9 liter V8

Classic grand tourer

This classic GT is fast, smooth and effortlessly stylish. Built to cruise at high speed, it's the James Bond of the car world.

Statistics

- **Top speed:** 150mph
- **0-60:** 8.4s
- **Horsepower:** 325hp
- **Engine:** 4 liter straight-6

Statistics

- **Top speed:** 90mph
- **0-60:** 14s
- **Horsepower:** 95hp
- **Engine:** 2.1 liter flat-4

Camper van

To catch the best waves you need to get off the beaten track. So strap on your boards, throw your wetsuit in the back and start chasing the surf!

Rally car

Rough, tough and agile, this four-wheel drive, turbo-charged machine is built to race down twisted dirt tracks.

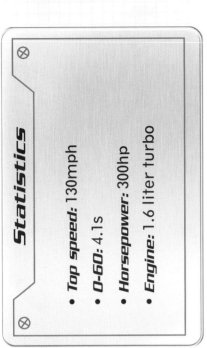

Statistics

- **Top speed:** 130mph
- **0-60:** 4.1s
- **Horsepower:** 300hp
- **Engine:** 1.6 liter turbo

Snow car

This arctic beast is perfectly adapted to its terrain. It tears across the snow on four caterpillar tracks, and runs on anti-freeze jet fuel.

Statistics

- **Top speed:** 75mph
- **0-60:** 13s
- **Horsepower:** 400hp
- **Engine:** 6.2 liter V8

Flatbed

Take the party on the road with this modified flatbed. It's the perfect machine for cruising down the beachfront, windows down and volume up.

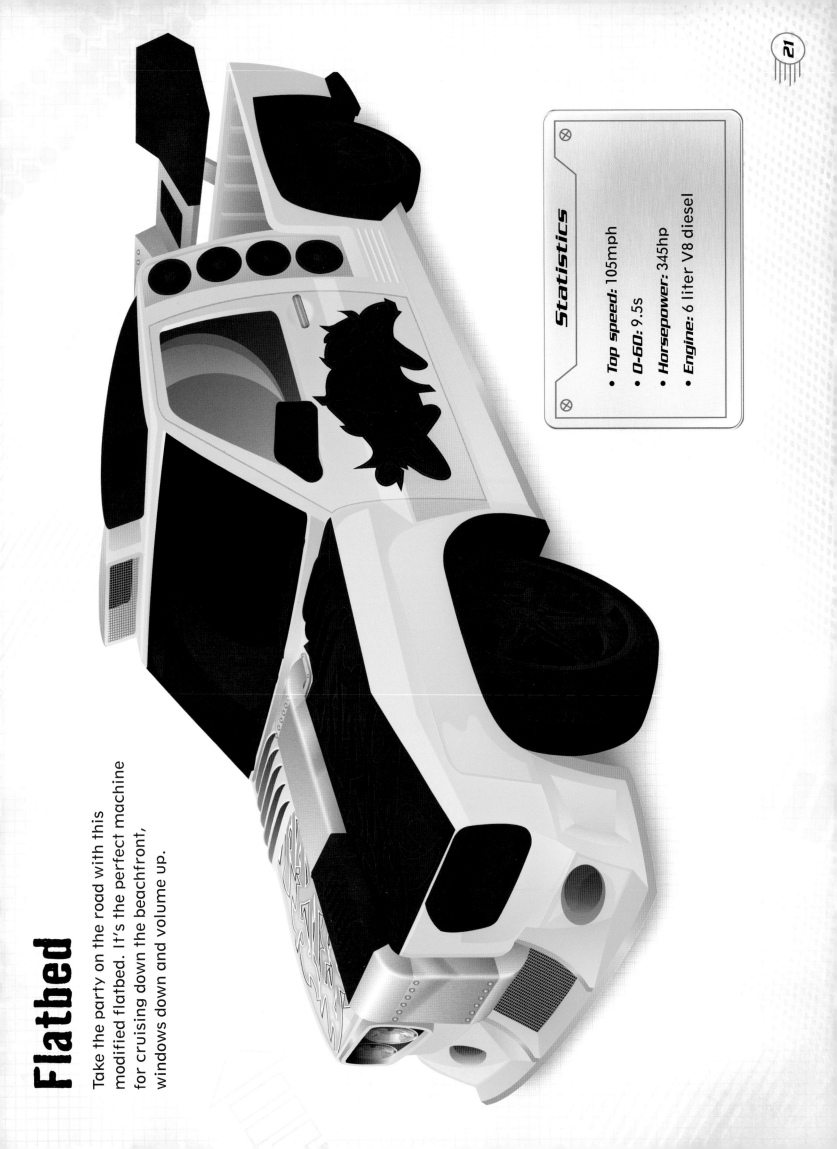

Statistics

- **Top speed:** 105mph
- **0-60:** 9.5s
- **Horsepower:** 345hp
- **Engine:** 6 liter V8 diesel

Top fuel dragster

This dragster is built for one thing and one thing only: speed. Running on purpose-made racing fuel, it accelerates like a jet on wheels.

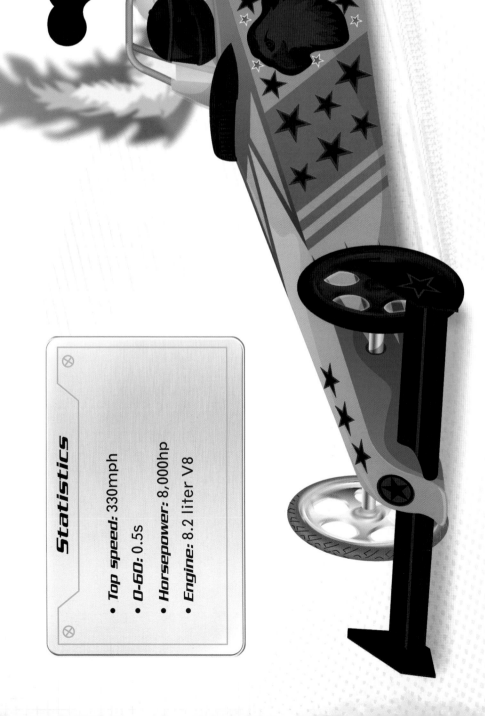

Statistics

- **Top speed:** 330mph
- **0-60:** 0.5s
- **Horsepower:** 8,000hp
- **Engine:** 8.2 liter V8

Car of the future

It's the year 2201. Cars float above the roads on magnetic fields, riding them like surfers on a wave. They sweep along so quietly that they play recordings of old gasoline engines, just to let people know they're coming.

Statistics

- **Top speed:** 200mph
- **0-60:** 3s
- **Horsepower:** n/a
- **Engine:** n/a

Glossary

- *accelerate:* speed up

- *automobile:* car

- *banked track:* a track that's tilted so one side is higher than the other. This means cars can go around corners faster.

- *convertible:* a car with a fold-down roof

- *diesel engine:* an engine that uses a type of fuel called diesel. Good for town cars and heavy vehicles, because it gives more power at low speeds.

- *drag car:* a car that's built for short races down a straight track

- *flat-4 engine:* an engine with four cylinders that are arranged in two pairs and laid out flat

- *four-wheel drive:* a vehicle where the engine powers all four wheels (normally only the front or back wheels are powered). Useful on rough terrain, when you can't rely on all the wheels having good contact with the ground.

- *horsepower (hp):* the power an engine is producing per second. The number in the statistics box is the maximum power that engine can produce.

- *km/h:* kilometres per hour

- *Le Mans Prototype:* a racing car designed for a 24-hour race in Le Mans, France

- *mph:* miles per hour

- *n/a:* not applicable (category doesn't apply)

- *NASCAR:* the National Association for Stock Car Auto Racing. NASCAR runs major stock car competitions in America.

- *Pro Mod:* a Pro Modified racer is a road car that's been turned into a drag racer

- *revving:* pressing the accelerator to increase the speed the engine is running. Drivers can rev their engines to make a quick start, by pressing the accelerator before the gears are engaged.

- *stock car:* a road car that's been modified for racing

- *straight-6 / straight-8 engine:* an engine with six or eight cylinders arranged in a straight line

- *supercharged engine:* an engine that uses compressed air to create more power

- *suspension:* a system of springs that lets the wheels of a vehicle move up and down without moving the whole vehicle. Deep suspension is needed for very bumpy terrain.

- *V6 / V8 / V12 engine:* an engine with six, eight or twelve cylinders arranged in two rows and angled in towards each other, forming a 'v' shape

Additional design by Reuben Barrance
Digital manipulation by Keith Furnival
Edited by Kirsteen Robson

First published in 2013 by Usborne Publishing Limited, 83-85 Saffron Hill, London EC1N 8RT, United Kingdom. usborne.com Copyright © 2013 Usborne Publishing Limited. The name Usborne and the Balloon logo are registered trade marks of Usborne Publishing Limited. All rights reserved. No part of this publication may be reproduced, stored in a retrieval system or transmitted in any form or by any means without prior permission of the publisher. First published in America 2013. This edition published 2023. AE

Super car page 2

185 MPH

SUPER CAR

SCREEECH!

Le Mans car page 3

24 hours

3

✽ These are extra stickers. Stick them wherever you like!

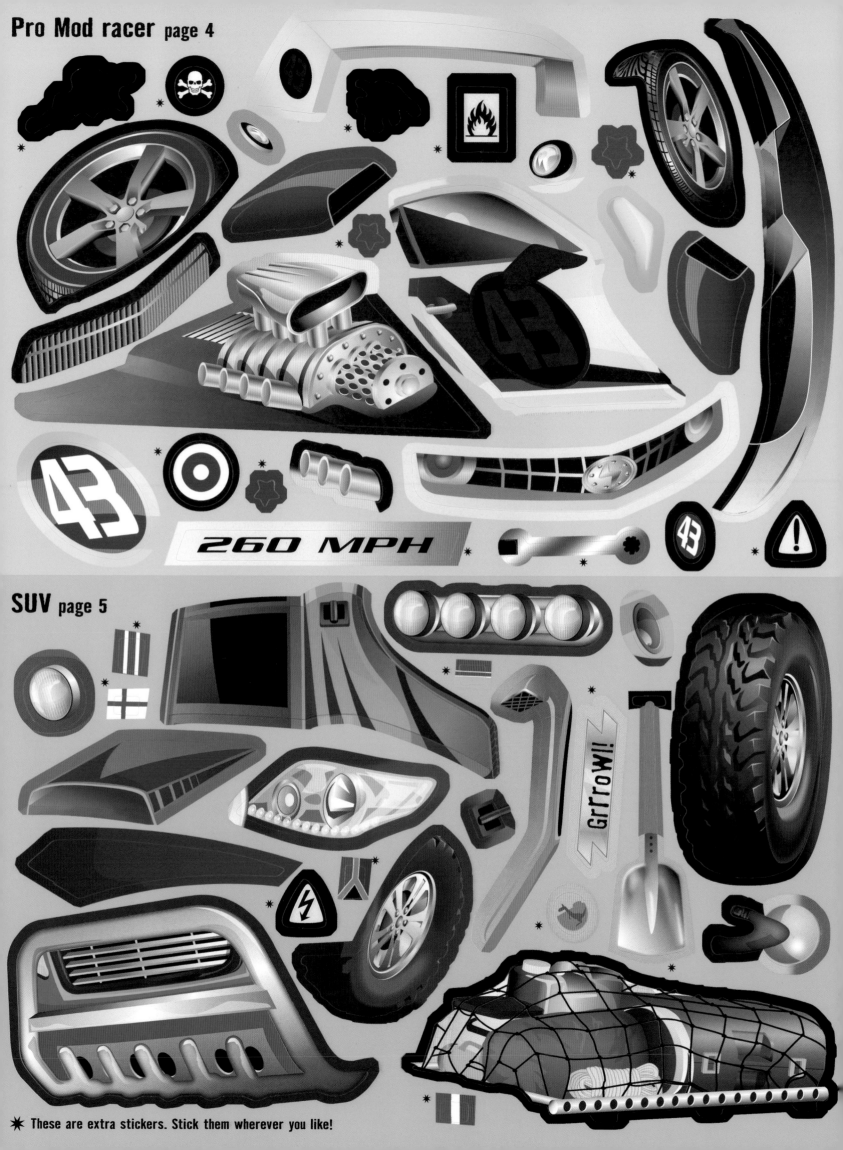

260 MPH

43

GrrroW!!

✶ These are extra stickers. Stick them wherever you like!